STEEL CITY PRE!

This first edition published in 2020 by Steel City Press,
9 Ravenscroft Close, Sheffield, S13 8PN.

ISBN 978-1-913047-10-8

Copyright © 2020 Jonathan Arnott

All rights reserved. This book or any portion thereof
may not be reproduced or used in any manner
whatsoever without the express written permission of
the publisher except for the use of brief quotations in a
book review.

Proudly printed in the United Kingdom.

All Scripture quotations, unless otherwise indicated, are taken from the Holy
Bible, New International Version®, NIV®. Copyright ©1973, 1978, 1984, 2011
by Biblica, Inc.™ Used by permission of Zondervan. All rights reserved worldwide.
www.zondervan.comThe "NIV" and "New International Version" are trademarks

registered in the United States Patent and Trademark Office by Biblica, Inc.™

# 40 DAYS IN THE DESERT

## (PRACTICAL CHRISTIANITY IN A TIME OF CHALLENGE)

By Jonathan Arnott

# INDEX

*"For I am convinced that neither death nor life, neither angels nor demons, neither the present nor the future, nor any powers, neither height nor depth, nor anything else in all creation, will be able to separate us from the love of God that is in Christ Jesus our Lord." - Romans 8 v 38 - 39*

# 40 Days in the desert

## (Practical Christianity in a time of challenge)

## Introduction

By the time you're reading this, I don't know what the situation will be. We're living in uncertain times.

As the COVID-19 virus spreads, churches across the country are stopping holding their Sunday services.

Any profits from the sale of this book will be used to help those affected by the outbreak.

I'm writing this to inspire Christians and churches around the country: now is the time for us as believers to unite (as a family of Christians around the globe), and to encourage us to take our responsibilities towards the wider world seriously.

This book is a series of daily devotionals, mainly (but not totally) focusing on how we can as Christians not just cope with the current situation, but thrive through it.

It is my fervent hope and prayer that through this situation, the church will be renewed and focused upon the things which matter. That is when the Kingdom of God will see exponential growth in our nation.

# DAY 1

## A ROYAL CHALLENGE

Esther was a Jewish exile who, against all the odds, became the Queen of Persia. The Jewish people were being persecuted. Mordecai a fellow Jew, asked Esther to take a stand and support her people. It was a risk, but Mordecai insisted (Esther 4 v 14) that God had a plan:

"For if you remain silent at this time, relief and deliverance for the Jews will arise from another place, but you and your father's family will perish. And who knows but that you have come to your royal position for such a time as this?" When Esther spoke up, her people were delivered. She risked her own life and saved the others.

As believers living in the New Testament, did you know that we are also royalty? 1 Peter 2 v 9 tells us that we are 'a Royal Priesthood'.

Maybe we have been placed here in this position 'for such a time as this'. Have you noticed how the church is becoming closer-knit, how we're in contact with each other on a daily basis and working out how we can help our community? It's building the conditions for an incredible, overwhelming move of God in the weeks and months ahead – but more on that another day.

# DAY 2

## GOD'S INCREDIBLE TIPPING POINT

Have you ever seen the 'penny shove' arcade machines at the seaside? Or if you're from a younger generation, the TV game show Tipping Point. The coin drops down lots of pegs, and then falls down onto a pile of coins which move backwards and forwards. Players keep putting pennies into the machine as the chain reaction continues, waiting for the tipping point - the moment when gravity pushes a load of coins over the final edge and the player wins them all at once. Of course, the game is rigged in the arcade's favour: on average, you get out fewer pennies than you put in.

Are you finding things difficult in these challenging times? The Bible also describes a kind of chain reaction in Romans 5 v 3-5: "We know that suffering produces perseverance; perseverance, character; and character, hope. And hope does not disappoint us."

When life is difficult, remember that with God's plan the chain reaction leads to something incredible: the hope of God, the hope that will never disappoint us.

# DAY 3

## WILL YOU OBEY GOD'S CALL?

*"Cleanse me with hyssop, and I shall be clean" – Psalm 51 v 7*

In the Old Testament, when God commanded His people to purify themselves using the branch of a hyssop tree and water, they had to obey. It must have seemed very strange to them. Thousands of years ago, people didn't even know about the basic necessity of doing simple things like washing our hands. They certainly didn't know that hyssop contains an antiseptic, thymol, which is the active ingredient in Listerine.

Through obedience to God's will, they protected themselves from disease – but they knew nothing of germs, so they just had to trust that God was right.

God might tell you to do something which doesn't make sense to our human minds. He might never reveal His reason or His plan, or he might reveal it long after we're gone. Will you still obey God, even when you can't see where that road is going to lead? And, as the government loves to say, don't forget to wash your hands!

# DAY 4

## TIME FOR OUR NATION TO PRAY?

"When I pray", said an old Archbishop of Canterbury William Temple, "concidences happen, and when I don't, they don't."

On May 26th 1940, during one of our nation's darkest hours in World War 2, King George called our nation to pray. Just days later, our troops were successfully evacuated from Dunkirk. In the August, the King called for young people to pray. Against all the odds, we survived the Battle of Britain. Then again, in March 1941, Hitler was planning to invade England. The nation was called to prayer. Yugoslavia had surrendered to the Nazis; it changed its mind. An earthquake and gales blew Nazi ships off course. Ethiopia was liberated from the Axis, and the British fleet destroyed the Italian fleet in the Mediterranean.

There were seven national days of prayer during World War 2; each was followed by tremendous victory. Coincidence? Or answer to prayer?

In 2 Chronicles 7 v 14, God promises "If my people, who are called by my name, will humble themselves and pray and seek my face and turn from their wicked ways, then I will hear from heaven, and I will forgive their sin and will heal their land".

When God makes a promise, He is faithful. Throughout this tough time, one thing we need more than anything else: national prayer.

# DAY 5

## SIMPLE CHRISTIANITY

Acts 2 v 44 – 47 describes the early church, telling us that "All the believers were together and had everything in common. They sold property and possessions to give to anyone who had need. Every day they continued to meet together in the temple courts. They broke bread in their homes and ate together with glad and sincere hearts, praising God and enjoying the favour of all the people."

It describes people's heart attitudes towards one another, and how those attitudes demonstrated something wonderful about Christianity. It doesn't mention evangelism, or sharing the Gospel. I'm sure that they must have been sharing the Gospel as well, because we're told to do that in the Great Commission. But the main characteristic of that early church was its complete and total rejection of the 'me me me' type of selfishness which has been so common.

When our heart attitude is right, God responds. Verse 47 finishes by saying "and the Lord added to their number daily those who were being saved". Is that what we want to see in our communities? Then our hearts must be right towards one another. I'm excited because I'm seeing this happen before my very eyes, but I want to challenge you today to do even more: to do what we're told in Philippians chapter 2 and 'in humility, put others before yourselves'.

# DAY 6

## WASHING YOUR HANDS (PART 1)

Acts 2 v 44 – 47 describes the early church, telling us that "All the believers were together and had everything in common. They sold property and possessions to give to anyone who had need. Every day they continued to meet together in the temple courts. They broke bread in their homes and ate together with glad and sincere hearts, praising God and enjoying the favour of all the people."

It describes people's heart attitudes towards one another, and how those attitudes demonstrated something wonderful about Christianity. It doesn't mention evangelism, or sharing the Gospel. I'm sure that they must have been sharing the Gospel as well, because we're told to do that in the Great Commission. But the main characteristic of that early church was its complete and total rejection of the 'me me me' type of selfishness which has been so common.

When our heart attitude is right, God responds. Verse 47 finishes by saying "and the Lord added to their number daily those who were being saved". Is that what we want to see in our communities? Then our hearts must be right towards one another. I'm excited because I'm seeing this happen before my very eyes, but I want to challenge you today to do even more: to do what we're told in Philippians chapter 2 and 'in humility, put others before yourselves'.

# DAY 7

## WASH YOUR HANDS (PART 2)

Why did Pontius Pilate wash his hands of Jesus? Why did he give in to the demands to put Jesus to death, even though he knew that the case against Jesus had neither legal nor moral merit? One word: fear. Pilate's job was on the line. He had upset the Jewish religious leaders too many times before. He knew that he was just one complaint to Rome away from being sacked as governor.

A bad tree brings forth bad fruit. Actions taken out of fear are usually bad ones. Pilate had Jesus crucified because he was scared. It didn't even save his job.

The historian Josephus records, in his book Antiquities of the Jews, that Pontius Pilate was sacked anyway after a later incident with the Samaritans. He was recalled to Rome in disgrace. History doesn't record whether he faced trial for his actions. We don't know what happened next. Perhaps he faced trial. Maybe he simply retired, or even committed suicide as the oral tradition goes. We do know that he never worked in a similar position again.

It's natural for us to feel fear, but there's an antidote to fear. You see, 1 John 4 v 18 tells us that "Perfect love casts out fear".

# DAY 8

## WASH YOUR HANDS (PART 3)

What do you do when you're washing your hands? That's 20 seconds of very valuable time. You could spend that time praying, or worshipping God. You're forming a habit by regularly spending the full 20 seconds with soap and water, but how about using that time to form another habit? The habit of spending time with God in prayer or in worship is one that it's so easy to forget in our modern world.

It's only 20 seconds regularly throughout the day, but it gives you a framework for making sure that you don't forget to pray or worship. There's a secular website www.washyourlyrics.com, which combines handwashing instructions with the lyrics of your favourite song. I suggest the wonderful Death Was Arrested by North Point Worship, which reminds us that our Lord has already won the victory over death. Isn't that an amazing inspirational thing to remind yourself of every single day?

# DAY 9

## DON'T PUT GOD INTO THE CORNER

"Nobody puts baby in a corner."

That's the most famous line from the film Dirty Dancing. It's become a phrase that people use when they're determined not to be left out of something.

Do we sometimes put God into a corner, allowing Him to only impact upon certain areas of our lives?

In chapter 5 v 13-18 of the book of James, we're reminded to let God into every part of our lives:

"Is anyone among you in trouble? Let them pray. Is anyone happy? Let them sing songs of praise. Is anyone among you sick? Let them call the elders of the church to pray over them and anoint them with oil in the name of the Lord. And the prayer offered in faith will make the sick person well; the Lord will raise them up. If they have sinned, they will be forgiven. Therefore confess your sins to each other and pray for each other so that you may be healed. The prayer of a righteous person is powerful and effective. Elijah was a human being, even as we are. He prayed earnestly that it would not rain, and it did not rain on the land for three and a half years. Again he prayed, and the heavens gave rain, and the earth produced its crops."

Don't put God into the corner. We shouldn't just talk to God when things are going wrong. If you're a parent, you want to hear about every part of your child's development. God is a perfect father. He wants to be involved in every part of our lives.

*If you have some time on your hands today, why not listen to 'Jesus be the Centre' by Michael Frye, and take a moment to put Him at the centre of your life where He should always be?*

# DAY 10

## BEING HONEST ABOUT WORRY

One of my friends keeps guinea pigs. They're wonderful animals, but always terrified. To soothe a guinea pig whilst holding it, you're supposed to put your hands over their eyes. When they can't see the thing they're worried about, guinea pigs soon calm down.

For many people, these are worrying times. You can't see a virus. You never know when it will strike. You might worry about yourself, or about your loved ones, about your church or nation or the whole world.

I'll let you into a secret: sometimes I struggle with worry, and putting my hands over my eyes (or my fingers in my ears) doesn't work as well for me as it does for a guinea pig. Don't get me wrong, I do know the Bible verses in my head. And I believe them.

2 Timothy 1 v 7 tells us that "God has not given us a spirit of fear, but of love, power and of a sound mind" [I like the NKJV translation here]. Matthew 6 v 25 – 27 says "Therefore I tell you, do not worry about your life, what you will eat or drink; or about your body, what you will wear. Is not life more than food, and the body more than clothes? Look at the birds of the air; they do not sow or reap or store away in barns, and yet your heavenly Father feeds them. Are you not much more valuable than they? Can any one of you by worrying add a single hour to your life?"

Those verses, and many more, are absolutely amazing. They remind us that God has kept us safe and secure in His wonderful, loving arms – and that we don't need to be frightened.

I think sometimes as Christians, we create a huge stigma around worry. Perhaps the worriers amongst us are reluctant to admit it, fearing that others in the church will think that our faith is somehow weak.

There's a risk that Christians feel too vulnerable to admit that they worry. Maybe they fear condemnation, but Romans 8 v 1 tells us that "[Therefore] there is no condemnation for those who are in Christ Jesus". Are you a worrier? Don't be ashamed to admit it.

Are you a mighty man or woman of faith who never worries about anything? Don't criticise the worriers. Instead, be there to stand side by side with them; help to lift them and build them up.

# DAY 11

## NO CHRISTIAN IS AN ISLAND

No man is an island, entire of itself. So said John Donne in his famous poem. Many people have been asked to self-isolate, to cut themselves off from the rest of society. Whether they are in an at-risk group, or have worrying symptoms, or have the COVID-19 virus, people are having to spend time on their own. As I write this, I'm thinking of countries in the world which have been placed on almost-complete lockdown. Perhaps by the time you read this, we'll be in the same situation.

Christianity isn't about being an island. We function as part of a body; we work together. The whole is supposed to be more than just the sum of its parts. As believers, there's something more about us: we're more than just the sum of our genes because we have the Spirit of the living God within us.

We also have technology. Pick up the phone. FaceTime someone who's lonely. Spend time with other believers online. Keep in touch by email. If you are able, drop a 'care package' on the doorstep of someone who's in need and having to self-isolate. Just because you're on lockdown doesn't mean you can't serve Jesus.

In Acts 16, Paul and Silas were in prison. They'd been flogged. Pause to think about that for a moment. Paul, a Roman citizen, had submitted himself to an illegal flogging. Why would he do that unless God had led him to do so, because God wanted him to be in prison for that night? They were in the most horrible cell, their feet in the stocks. What were they doing?

Verse 25 tells us that "About midnight Paul and Silas were praying and singing hymns to God, and the other prisoners were listening to them". Wow! What faith! You might know the rest of the story. An earthquake set them free, but they chose to remain in prison. By doing so, they were able to bring the jailer and his entire family to Christ.

Adversity turned into triumph is the very DNA of Christianity. Are you on lockdown? Be inspired by Paul and Silas. To misquote John Donne, ask not for whom the bell tolls. It can never toll for a believer.

# DAY 12

## THE MOST DIFFICULT QUESTIONS

I've seen people prayed for, who were supernaturally healed of an illness by the power of God. I've prayed for people myself and seen healing. Yet Christians still get sick. We don't know God's plans, and can't explain why one person is healed and another not.

We also have a medical profession. It would be completely irresponsible to simply assume that God will do what we want, and permit the consequences of that to happen. If I have an asthma attack, I'm going to use my inhaler. I'm not saying that I wouldn't or shouldn't pray (or that I shouldn't thank God for the fact that we have the healthcare that we do). But if I refused to use the inhaler and just prayed, presuming that God must then answer my prayer, it would be putting my own will above His.

When we respond as Christians to COVID-19, we remember that we have a spiritual responsibility. We're supposed to model for the world a way to live our lives.

# DAY 13

## FAKE NEWS

Did you know that the Bible warned us about fake news, two thousand years ago? Matthew 24 v 24 tells us about that "false messiahs and false prophets will appear and perform great signs and wonders to deceive, if possible, even the elect". From Ahab to Zedekiah, the Bible tells us about false prophets – and warns us that there will be more to come.

1 John 4 warns us not to believe "every spirit, but test the spirits to see whether they are from God, because many false prophets have gone out into the world".

What does testing mean? It's an important spiritual principle, repeated in 1 Thessalonians 5 v 18. First, we test what we hear against the Bible – if it's from God, it'll fit with His Word. Second, we test it in prayer: ask God, and listen to the response in our spirit. Third, test it against common sense.

Fake news abounds. Fake news about COVID-19 can kill because it tells people to do the wrong things in response. Don't share anything on social media unless you've checked first that it's true, and considered whether it's right to share it. That applies to the whole of our lives, not just to this.

Ridiculous predictions of a level of cataclysm far beyond that suggested by the evidence will merely spread fear, but downplaying the current situation would lead to the kind of complacency which could ultimately spread the virus further and lead to more people dying.

We should be reasonable in everything we do.

*Today, please pray for protection of our society against the spread of fake news - whether it's done maliciously or with the best of intentions.*

# DAY 14

## CHRISTIANS MUST OBEY GOD

## (BUT THAT HAS A WIDER MEANING)

Are you reading this, sitting there in utter frustration because you don't want to comply with the current restrictions on your movement? Do you want to go against government advice and instructions, running a risk either to yourself or to the community?

Tension and frustration are undoubtedly running pretty high in these times. I'm sorry if this comes across as being harsh, but if you disobey the government's health advice at a time like this then you're also being disobedient to God.

Our instructions from God come from the Bible. Just a reminder: 2 Timothy 3 v 16 tells us that "all Scripture is God-breathed and is useful for teaching, rebuking, correcting and training in righteousness". There's no wiggle room on this.

Romans 13 v 1 - 5 is blunt and direct. It's the Word of God, and there's no getting around it:

"Let everyone be subject to the governing authorities, for there is no authority except that which God has established. The authorities that exist have been established by God. Consequently, whoever rebels against the authority is rebelling against what God has instituted, and those who do so will bring judgment on themselves. For rulers hold no terror for those who do right, but for those who do wrong. Do you want to be free from fear of the one in authority? Then do what is right and you will be commended. For the one in authority is God's servant for your good. But if you do wrong, be afraid, for rulers do not bear the sword for no reason. They are God's servants, agents of wrath to bring punishment on the wrongdoer. Therefore, it is necessary to submit to the authorities, not only because of possible punishment but also as a matter of conscience."

Governments don't always get things right. In a democracy, we have the right to criticise reasonably and rationally when we think they're making a mistake. But we don't have the selfish luxury of ignoring what's expected of us.

# DAY 15

## KEEP GOING - GOD WILL PROVIDE!

At home, we have a gas fireplace. Turn the dial, and a small pilot light will click into action. It doesn't always work the first time. Sometimes it goes out, and we have to turn the dial again. We might have to do it three or four times before it suddenly bursts into flames, and the whole fire is lit.

A fire starts with a single spark. Sometimes it feels like that's all we've got, that we're living on a spark. It's easy for us to start to feel down about it. But Isaiah 42 v 3 tells us "A bruised reed he will not break, and a smoldering wick he will not snuff out."

If you're feeling that way, like all you have left is a spark or a little pilot light in your life, remember that you're not on your own at all. God provides the gas – and it can become a blazing fire faster than you could possibly imagine.

# DAY 16

## ARE YOU DOING YOUR UTMOST?

At the age of 13, John Byng joined the Royal Navy. He served his country faithfully for 30 years, rising to the rank of Vice Admiral and becoming a Member of Parliament.

As an admiral he was ordered to relieve a besieged British garrison in Minorca, but given a fleet of ships in poor repair. He failed to beat the French fleet. Instead of trying again, he headed to Gibraltar to refit his ships.

He was court-martialled and executed by firing squad for 'failing to do his utmost' to defeat the enemy. But for a century after that, British admirals were so terrified of meeting Byng's fate that they would attack relentlessly when faced with the enemy.

The French philosopher Voltaire said that in England, they like to shoot an admiral from time to time to encourage the others.

What happened to Byng was unfair. We do not have an unfair judge, but a fair one. Luke 18 v 6 – 8 says this: "And will not God bring about justice for his chosen ones, who cry out to him day and night? Will he keep putting them off? I tell you, he will see that they get justice, and quickly."

Still, we must face judgement when we die. What's the standard that we hold ourselves to? Did we do the bare minimum for salvation?

Or can we stand before our God and say we did our utmost, leaving no stone unturned because of our passion for the lost?

That's the challenge.

*Today, please pray to ask God to show you what His will is for you today. What difference can you make during such a time as this?*

# DAY 17

## BELIEVE IN YOURSELF - YOU'VE BEEN TRANSFORMED!

Eugène François Vidocq was a petty criminal until he turned his life around and started working for the police. His detective work became the inspiration for Sherlock Holmes.

What a transformation! From criminal to inspiring the most famous fictional detective ever. Do you know what? That transformation is NOTHING to the transformation in your life, when you went from lost to saved through the power of Jesus Christ!

The famous hymn Amazing Grace tells us that "I once was lost, but now am found; was blind, but now I see". There can be no greater transformation than the one which took place in your heart.

Isn't that something amazing, something to inspire confidence in these trying times? 2 Corinthians 5 v 17 tells us "Therefore, if anyone is in Christ, the new creation has come: The old has gone, the new is here!"

# DAY 18

## EVERY CONTACT LEAVES A TRACE

I recently heard Carl Beech giving a talk, where he described how his father had been a detective. One time, they caught a criminal because of microscopic specks of blood on her glasses. Another time, the dust on a criminal's trousers matched the dust at the scene of a crime. DNA evidence may not even be visible to the naked eye, but it's still there. Every contact leaves a trace.

John 13 v 34 says this: "By this shall all men know that you are my disciples, that you love one another as I have first loved you."

Don't be discouraged when you show God's abundant love, in practical ways, to those around you who aren't believers - and they're not saved immediately. Every contact leaves a trace. It may take days, weeks, months, or even years - but those contacts will show them that there's something different about us. That we're different. Why? Because we are Christians, and He who is in us is greater than He who is in the world.

*How can you show practical love for those in your community (both believers and unbelievers) today?*

# DAY 19

## WHAT REALLY MATTERS

A while ago, I had occasion to visit a cathedral in a Catholic country. Tourists were gushing about the architecture, the art...all the trappings, in face they loved everything yet missed what it's all meant to be about: God. When Christianity fails to focus on Christ, it's like a child's toy with the batteries taken out. Forget the fancy stuff that we create with our human effort; remember the eternal stuff. God. All those people walking through a building meant for the worship of God seemed totally oblivious to God himself.

If there's one thing I believe that God is teaching the church during the current crisis, it's this. We can't necessarily meet together on a Sunday, but the church was never supposed to be fixated on the building. Now we're being forced to think of church more in terms of the people, we're starting to see a mighty move of God.

Forget the buildings. Forget the architecture. Forget personal possessions and creature comforts. Instead, follow Psalm 37 v 4: "Delight yourself in the Lord and He will give you the desires of your heart."

It's not handing God a wish-list and expecting Him to comply with your desires. It's about delighting yourself in the Lord because the moment you do that, the desires of your heart become better matched to God's will.

# DAY 20

## WHO DO YOU TRUST?

Psalm 20 v 7 says "Some trust in chariots and some in horses, but we trust in the name of the Lord our God."

The chariot is a symbol of opulence. The world trusts the finer human things of life, even though we are living through a time when we might be denied those things. The horse is symbolic of might and military power. Through cavalry, whole kingdoms were subdued. In the current time, it's easy to put our trust in science, in the development of treatments and vaccines.

No, that's not what we're called to do. We're out of step with a world obsessed with materialism over spirituality. As the Christian solo artist Bianca puts it, we march to the beat of a different drum. John 15 v 19 explains it like this: "If you belonged to the world, it would love you as its own. As it is, you do not belong to the world, but I have chosen you out of the world. That is why the world hates you".

Today, I urge you to spend a little time in prayer – and ensure that your focus is on the right things. Not horses, or chariots, or anything else that could distract us from our Lord.

# DAY 21

## THE INCREDIBLE IMPORTANCE OF WORSHIP

Many churches have embraced new ideas and new technology in recent weeks. If people cannot go to church, then we must bring church to them.

One simple idea has been to live-stream services on the internet. A Sunday service can be run with just a worship team (two metres apart for safety) and a preacher.

How does that help those people within the congregation who have no internet and must self-isolate? We can find ways around that too: a DVD (and a portable DVD player if necessary), or telephoning them during the service so that they can listen?

Nothing's going to stop us worshipping God together. In the Bible, when the disciples worshipped God and thanked Him for the miracles which He had done, unsurprisingly the Pharisees were upset. They were more concerned with decorum than giving God the glory for his actions. They asked Jesus to rebuke His disciples. Jesus responded (Luke 19 v 40): "I tell you, if they remain silent, the very stones will cry out."

As human beings, we are designed to worship. Even unbelievers often worship, but instead of worshipping God they worship a strange assortment of musicians, footballers, actors and celebrities.

There's an imperative: worshipping God must happen. It's not optional. If the disciples didn't do so, the very stones would cry out and worship God. Even if we should be in a position where half a dozen of us couldn't meet to live-stream a church service, we could and would continue to worship from home.

Let's give God all the glory. Right here. Right now.

# DAY 22

## DO NUMBERS MATTER?

Throughout the Bible, you'll see the same numbers occurring over and over again. The numbers 7 and 12 are symbolic, referring to Jewishness. The number 144 crops up frequently (because it is 12 multiplied by 12).

Jacob had 12 sons, becoming the 12 tribes of Israel. Jesus had 12 disciples and it's no coincidence that when He fed the five thousand, there were 12 baskets left over. The number 3 speaks of the Trinity: God the Father, God the Son and God the Holy Spirit. Three, and yet one: the nature of God which our human minds cannot even comprehend.

My mind keeps being drawn back to small numbers today. Ecclesiastes 4 tells us that whilst one person can be overpowered, two can defend themselves. We can watch each other's back. If one falls down, the other can help them up. Two people lying down together can keep each other warm.

We're reminded that a three-fold cord is not easily broken. Think of a rope created by weaving two strands together. It will be unstable, but if you add a third strand then it will hold almost any weight you might want it to bear.

These are all, of course, metaphors for people. We don't need to be an American-style huge church of tens of thousands to have the presence of God.

Whilst we're not meeting together in large gatherings, Jesus tells us in Matthew 18 v 20 that "where two or three gather in my name, there am I with them". His presence is not dependent upon huge numbers. His presence depends upon our hearts.

It's important to encourage one another and to lift each other up. We shouldn't be fully isolated; even if we have to self-isolate we can stay in touch by phone or online. Large numbers don't matter, but friendship and accountability does.

# DAY 23

## THE BLANK PAGE

Turn to the very start of the book of Matthew in your Bible. Then, go back one page. In most Bibles, that's an empty page – a placeholder, if you will, between the Old Testament and the New Testament. One of the best (and certainly most memorable) sermons I've heard in the last year took the blank page as its text.

At the very end of the Old Testament, the book of Malachi prophesies the coming of Jesus Christ. We don't know the exact date it was written, but most likely it was 400 years before Jesus was born.

People who were alive during the time of the prophet Malachi, excited in anticipation by his words, would not live to see those prophesies come to pass. Instead, the Jewish people waited for centuries for their Saviour. And even when Jesus came, the religious leaders of the day could not recognise that Saviour.

Imagine that period of frustration, of waiting, hoping for the fulfilment of the prophecy. If there's one thing I find more difficult in my Christian walk than anything else, it's waiting. When God makes a promise, He will never break His word. Don't expect that you can choose the timing though. Psalm 27 tells us that we should wait 'patiently' for the Lord.

Waiting can be difficult: waiting for a job offer, waiting for a diagnosis, waiting for life to return to normal. Yet almost every major figure in the Bible had to wait at one time or another. Abraham had to wait 25 years to see God's promises come to pass. Joseph went to prison. Waiting is a part of our Christian walk with God, and it's never an easy one.

Are we able to wait for God's perfect timing? Or do we sometimes end up asking 'God, grant me patience – and I want it right now'? Perhaps God is teaching you something about waiting. Maybe that is part of His plan.

# DAY 24

## THE 7,000

When Elijah was hiding in a cave, he complained to God. In 1 Kings 19 v 14, he said "I have been very zealous for the Lord God Almighty. The Israelites have rejected your covenant, torn down your altars, and put your prophets to death with the sword. I am the only one left, and now they are trying to kill me too."

Elijah was feeling at the end of his tether. He was looking for God to answer his prayers, to be able to understand that age-old problem: the reality of his situation in the physical world didn't match the promises of God. He was alone, and he was scared. But he wasn't the only one. He wasn't alone: God tells him in verse 18 "I reserve seven thousand in Israel—all whose knees have not bowed down to Baal and whose mouths have not kissed him".

We often think of this from the point of view of Elijah. We imagine ourselves being the one hiding in the cave, and even though we don't know it yet, God has support and provisions ready for us. That's true.

Now imagine you're one of the 7,000. Imagine God has set you aside for the purpose of supporting the prophet Elijah. And he's hiding in a cave, terrified. It's so easy, isn't it, to start to take a negative view of our leaders? The pastor of your local church probably isn't hiding in a cave at the moment, but criticism of those in authority is pretty common. The list of mistakes made by the prophets and kings of the Bible is pretty horrific: even the great King David was a murderer and adulterer.

In this difficult time, it's entirely possible that your church leaders may not be absolutely perfect. They're human beings, with struggles, just like everybody else. Zechariah 13 v 7 tells us "Strike the shepherd, and the sheep will be scattered". Your leaders may well come under a sustained period of spiritual attack. They need you in their corner, not sniping against every bad decision.

I'd urge you today: be one of the 7,000. Offer every help to the leadership of your church as they do their best to navigate us through this difficult time.

# DAY 25

## MY LIGHTHOUSE

One of my friends completely ruined the Rend Collective song 'My Lighthouse' for me.

It's a lovely song: *My lighthouse, my lighthouse. Shining in the darkness, I will follow You. My lighthouse, my lighthouse. I will trust the promise. You will carry me safe to shore.*

Wonderful words, aren't they? Especially when you see children and young people working out a series of actions to a catchy, quirky tune. Except my friend pointed out a rather basic fact. That's not what a lighthouse does. A lighthouse is there so that ships know to steer clear, to avoid hitting the shore. It's a light warning us to steer clear of danger.

Matthew 5 v 14 tells us that we are the light of the world. Psalm 119 v 105 tells us that God's word is a lamp for our feet.

God's light actually serves both functions. When we walk in God's light, we can see sin clearly. It is a lighthouse, telling us to keep away from the rocks of sin. It's also a light for our feet, helping to guide us safely to the place where He wants us to be.

A while ago, I had the opportunity to visit Iceland with my wife. We went out of the city of Reykjavik in search of the Northern Lights. We had to leave the city to seek them, because otherwise the glow of the city would get in the way. If you sometimes feel, like Elijah did, that you're the only one around who's standing tall for your faith in Jesus Christ, remember this. When it's dark, even a small light can be seen for miles around.

Don't despair if you can't see any other lights today. Instead, rejoice that your light will be visible to many!

# DAY 26

## CHRISTIANS DON'T GIVE UP

Do you remember the Chumbawumba song 'I get knocked down, but I get up again'? That song always reminds me of 2 Corinthians 4 v 8 – 9.

Those verses tell us that "We are hard pressed on every side, but not crushed; perplexed, but not in despair; persecuted, but not abandoned; struck down, but not destroyed". The Bible doesn't promise us that every day of our Christian walk will be a 'walk in the park'. Instead, it promises that we'll face trials and tribulations. Just look at the Apostle Paul: he was beaten with rods, shipwrecked, flogged, stoned, imprisoned and in danger everywhere he went.

The Christian walk isn't supposed to be easy. But Christians don't give up. I don't mean that in some macho sense. I'm not telling you to 'pull yourself together' and everything will be fine. No, I'm telling you that God also has a promise for us.

He will let us go through times which are difficult. An athlete trains by pushing themselves to the very limit because that's the way they'll get the maximum possible performance from their body. Similarly, we will be pushed and tried and tested – and through that, we'll come to a deeper faith in God.

So where is God's promise? It's in 1 Corinthians 10 v 13, in which we learn that however difficult things might be He will not push us beyond our breaking point: "No temptation has overtaken you except what is common to mankind. And God is faithful; he will not let you be tempted beyond what you can bear. But when you are tempted, he will also provide a way out so that you can endure it."

Whatever your struggles, stand on the promises of God and you **will** get through them.

# DAY 27

## GOD'S INCREDIBLE PLAN

Have you ever heard the phrase 'good things come to those who wait'? You probably have: it's not only a common saying, it's also been used to advertise everything from baked beans to Guinness.

Have you ever heard someone discuss Jeremiah 29 v 11? "For I know the plans I have for you," declares the Lord, "plans to prosper you and not to harm you, plans to give you hope and a future". It's one of the most well-known verses in the Bible; I can't imagine there are many people who've been a Christian for very long without having seen it. It's a wonderful feeling, to know that God has a perfect plan for our lives.

Strangely enough, the verse immediately before it (Jeremiah 29 v 10) isn't quite so well known: "When seventy years are completed for Babylon, I will come to you and fulfil my good promise to bring you back to this place".

The thought of God's plans for our future is much more popular than the thought of having to wait for 70 years for those plans to come into fruition. If you feel like you're waiting for God's plans, don't sit around doing nothing. Use the time constructively instead.

# DAY 28

## OUR FATHER

Today, I'm thinking about prayer. I wonder how often we actually do prayer 'correctly' as Christians? Prayer isn't a wish-list. Prayer isn't a tick-box exercise.

But what actually should we be doing when we pray? Older people in our society will still remember the Lord's Prayer, word for word, from learning it at school.

But why did Jesus give us the Lord's Prayer in the first place? It was in response to a question from His disciples, asking Him to teach us how to pray. If there's a template for prayer, anywhere in the Bible, then that template is found in the Lord's Prayer. Today, I'd like to just focus on the first two words of the Lord's Prayer.

***Our Father...***

God is our Father. Our earthly parents may have been exceptional, or they may have been awful. We all have different experiences of parents.

But just like nobody can live their lives without sin, no earthly parent is perfect. God is the perfect Father, able to do "immeasurably more than we ask or imagine" according to Ephesians 3 v 20.

When we come to God in prayer, we need to remember that He is our father. Just like a child would approach their parent, we should approach God with directness and simplicity.

Right at the start of the prayer, we're reminding ourselves of His role in our development.

A parent nurtures their children, helping them to grow into the best person that they can possibly be.

When we pray 'Our Father', we take the focus away from the worldly idea that we're just 'asking God for more stuff'. We put the emphasis back on where it should be: on our own development rather than our human desires.

# DAY 29

## FAITH

Other than the Bible, the most widely-read book in Christianity is a fifteenth-century work by Thomas à Kempis, entitled The Imitation of Christ.

Ephesians 5 v 1 tells us to be "imitators of God", and that was modelled for us by Jesus Christ himself.

It's easy for Christians to fall into the trap of thinking in very simple terms about a 'vengeful' Old Testament God, and a 'gentle' New Testament Jesus Christ. We're told that God is the same yesterday, today and forever. There is a difference between the Old Covenant and the New Covenant of course, but we still worship (as the Matt Redman song points out) the same Jesus today.

In Mark 11 v 15 we are told that "On reaching Jerusalem, Jesus entered the temple courts and began driving out those who were buying and selling there. He overturned the tables of the money changers and the benches of those selling doves, and would not allow anyone to carry merchandise through the temple courts. And as he taught them, he said, "Is it not written: 'My house will be called a house of prayer for all nations'? But you have made it 'a den of robbers.'"

Those people who incurred Jesus' anger in that situation were attempting to profit from worshippers going to the temple. That kind of exploitative attitude is something which should have no place in our hearts, and we - like Jesus - should protect others from it.

When Jesus saw injustice, he fought it and stood up for justice. The theme of justice (no modifier necessary) is consistent throughout the Bible.

The COVID-19 outbreak has led to all kinds of social reactions. Some people have responded in the most amazing, public-spirited ways. Others have been exploitative, seeking to profit from the suffering of others.

As Christians, there's nothing wrong with challenging anyone who is seen to be exploiting others. We should be there to help the needy and the vulnerable in society. That doesn't mean going off like a firework every time we see something we dislike, of course, but it does mean that we should be fiercely protective of those who are most in need.

# DAY 30

## STOCKPILING

Here's a tough question faced by many Christians at the moment. When people have stockpiled food and essential supplies in an attempt to see themselves through the COVID-19 outbreak, how should we respond?

There are examples in the Bible of storehouses, making sure that there is plenty of food in order to be able to prepare for famine. In Genesis 41, Joseph interprets Pharaoh's dream to mean that there would be seven years of plenty followed by seven years of famine. By building up stores during those years, they were not only able to provide their own needs but to help others as well.

That's a slightly different situation. Christians rushing to panic-buy every last toilet roll in the supermarket wouldn't have been such a good idea either. Why? Because it would have deprived others - possibly those more vulnerable - of essential items.

During a time of plenty, it's reasonable to put something aside to make sure that you're going to be okay later. In fact, you could even go so far as to say that it's good stewardship.

During a time when supplies have been limited, we shouldn't competitively buy more than we need for ourselves - unless the reason is that we're buying in order to donate it (for example to a neighbour or to the local foodbank).

I understand that some people, who won't be able to go out to the supermarkets, needed to make sure that they had enough food to last them in the short term.

It's all about common sense: are we doing things with the right heart? Is it the 'I want, I want' selfishness of the human nature - or is it the Biblical principle of good stewardship for ourselves and the community? We need to be honest with ourselves.

But we're instructed that we should do a different kind of stockpiling too. Matthew 6 v 19 - 21 says ""Do not store up for yourselves treasures on earth, where moths and vermin destroy, and where thieves break in and steal. But store up for yourselves treasures in heaven, where moths and vermin do not destroy, and where thieves do not break in and steal. For where your treasure is, there your heart will be also."

Are you stockpiling your treasure in heaven, or are you purely focused on this earth?

# DAY 31

## ONCE IN A CENTURY

*"Stand firm, ye boys from Maine, for not once in a century are men permitted to bear such responsibility for freedom and justice, for God and humanity as are now placed upon you."*

Those were the inspirational words of Colonel Joshua Lawrence Chamberlain at the Battle of Gettysburg. The Union Army was in danger of being overrun. If they did not hold the hill at Little Round Top, defeat was certain. But to attempt to hold the hill would lead to certain death.

Instead, Colonel Chamberlain chose another course of action. They charged down the hill directly at the enemy, taking them by surprise. Chamberlain himself was shot twice during the battle, and awarded the U.S. Medal of Honor for his bravery.

Chamberlain was a university lecturer. He wasn't a professional soldier before the American Civil War broke out, but he served his country with distinction in its hour of need.

We're facing a once-in-a-century crisis as a nation. Not since the Spanish flu pandemic of 1918 has there been such a severe threat in peacetime. The world is changing.

As the world is changing, there's a generational opportunity for us: for individual Christians and for whole churches.

Am I contradicting myself here? How can this be both a time of waiting and a time of great excitement about how God is moving?

I think it's both at the same time. Think about the way that the virus is spreading within our communities. When the virus is passed on, you don't get the symptoms straight away. There's an 'incubation period' as it grows within the body.

Look at it from one perspective, and it seems like nothing is happening. From a different perspective, all the groundwork is being done.

Now apply that to church. Maybe we're in an 'incubation period'. Perhaps we're waiting, but we're waiting in such a way that brings congregations closer together.

Ephesians 4 v 3-6 tells us to "Make every effort to keep the unity of the Spirit through the bond of peace. There is one body and one Spirit, just as you were called to one hope when you were called; one Lord, one faith, one baptism; one God and Father of all, who is over all and through all and in all."

***Today, why not listen to an old song: 'They'll know we are Christians' by Carolyn Arends? The church in our nation needs to be as one.***

# DAY 32

## HOPE DOES NOT DISAPPOINT

*"We know that suffering produces perseverance; perseverance,*
*character; and character, hope. And hope does not disappoint us"*
*- Romans 3 v 3 - 5*

No, this isn't a typo! I know we've used this passage already in this series, but I really want to focus back on that word: hope. It's a critical word for where we're at now.

In 1732, Alexander Pope first used the phrase 'hope springs eternal'. Doesn't that poetic phrase inspire confidence in you? Doesn't it show how hope can spread from deep within?

The word 'hope' in the English language has been watered down. I studied Spanish many years ago, and learned that the verb 'esperar' means both 'to hope' and 'to expect'. The word 'hope' carried with it a form of belief that something is going to happen.

If someone says 'I hope that my local football team win today', it doesn't inspire confidence. It's not a prediction or expectation (especially if that team happens to be Scunthorpe United) of victory, but just an indication of something that you desire to happen.

When the Bible talks of hope, it's the non-watered-down version. The Ancient Greek (and Hebrew) words both in themselves convey that idea of expectation.

Romans 8 v 24 - 25 tells us a little more about hope: "For in hope we have been saved, but hope that is seen is not hope; for why does one also hope for what he sees? But if we hope for what we do not see, with perseverance we wait eagerly for it."

Don't think of Biblical hope like it's a random, uncontrollable event (I hope that it won't rain this afternoon). Think of hope as something you're sure of.

Faith and hope are powerfully linked. They can never disappoint us because God keeps His promises. He will never let us down.

# DAY 33

## YOU'RE NEVER REJECTED

*"The stone the builders rejected has become the cornerstone"* - *Psalm 118 v 22*

This world is all messed up. It's got every priority wrong. It considers things like money, power, beauty and celebrity to be more important than almost everything else.

It's so mixed up that when God himself came down to earth, the world completely and utterly rejected Him.

The biggest Empire the world had ever seen, the Roman Empire, rejected Him. The Jewish religious leaders rejected Him. Some of his own people judged Him because of his background, lack of status and wealth. Even one of His own disciples, who had followed Him for years, denied knowing him when the going got tough.

If this world even rejected Jesus, why are we so keen to seek its acceptance? Don't get me wrong, there's absolutely nothing wrong with spending time with non-believers. How else will they see that there's something different about Christians? But we don't need the world to put us on a pedestal. We don't need to comply with their definitions of success.

There's a wonderful Rich Mullins song entitled 'Homeless Man', inspired by Luke 9 v 58 which says "Foxes have dens and birds have nests, but the Son of Man has no place to lay his head."

Rich Mullins' lyrics are poetic, but they're inspirational. It finishes with these words:

*Birds have nests, foxes have dens*
*But the hope of the whole world rests*
*On the shoulders of a homeless man*
*You had the shoulders of a homeless man*
*And the world can't stand what it can't own*
*And it can't own You*
*'Cause You did not have a home*

If you're rejected by this world because you've chosen to follow God, then it's straightforward: God is right; the world is in the wrong. You're never rejected when you're living God's way.

Human beings might reject you, but never forget that you're the cornerstone of His plan for your life.

# DAY 34

## SHE SAID YES

The title of today's devotional is taken from the story of Cassie Bernall*, an (extra-) ordinary American teenager from Colorado who happened to be a Christian.

Picture the scene: you're a teenage girl going to school just like you do every other day. You'd dabbled with drugs and alcohol, but after going on a Christian retreat your life changed. You're laughing with your friends, hoping you've obtained a good mark on your recent homework assignments, and making plans for the weekend. Nothing's special about this day or any other day.

Except, the school you attend is Columbine High School - and it's April 20, 1999. Two students burst into the school, armed with guns and home-made bombs. They start to open fire.

You hide under a table, hoping to save your life. One of the shooters sees you, and hears you mention the word God. A gun is pointed to your face, and you're asked whether you believe in God.

If you say 'No', you have a chance of being allowed to live. If you say 'Yes', you expect to die immediately. How do you respond?

We'd all like to be able to say 'Yes', but it's difficult when you've not been in that situation. The band Petra grappled with this issue in their song 'If I had to die for someone'.

Would you be able to give up your life on account of your faith in our Lord Jesus Christ? For one teenage girl, that question turned from hypothetical to real in a matter of seconds.

Maybe it's felt more like that to us recently, given the state of the COVID-19 outbreak. We want to protect ourselves, but to help others. It's difficult to know where sensible precautions end, and where selfishness begins.

Our medical professionals put their lives on their line for us on a daily basis. Let's make sure to remember them in all of our prayers.

Romans 5 v 7 - 8 says this: "Very rarely will anyone die for a righteous person, though for a good person someone might possibly dare to die. But God demonstrates his own love for us in this: While we were still sinners, Christ died for us."

What an incredible sacrifice he made!

* - *Some witnesses claim it was actually a different student who answered that question with 'Yes'. The story is equally inspirational either way.*

# DAY 35

## NEVER FORGET THE PERSECUTED CHURCH

A while ago, when I was asked to speak on the subject 'Healthy Christians are Free', my first thought went to those Christians who live behind bars or who are in captivity because of their faith.

At the time of writing, Leah Sharibu is still alive. She's one of two hundred teenagers who were kidnapped by the Boko Haram militant group in Nigeria.

After years of being held captive, the girls were asked to put on a hijab and read an Islamic declaration of faith.

Leah Sharibu is not a Muslim. She is a Christian. The other girls begged her to just 'say the words' and secure her release, but she refused to do so.

The other girls were all released, but Leah Sharibu remains in captivity even today.

What stubbornness! But also, what a witness to her captors! Such refusal to 'say the words' is likely to have a profound effect, because it shows that her faith is real - even when it comes at a personal price.

I think at this time, we're at risk of becoming quite insular. How easy it is, when things are difficult here, for us to forget about all of the other situations in which people are worse off than ourselves.

More than 10% of Christians around the world are persecuted for their faith. We should not forget them in our prayers, nor forget the amazing work done by charities like Open Doors and the Barnabas Fund.

John 8 v 36 says "So if the Son sets you free, you will be free indeed". Many people have been imprisoned for their faith in Jesus over the 2,000 years since He said those words.

They're still free. And we're still free.

*Today, why not listen to the song Who You Say I Am - by Hillsong Worship? Let's celebrate that we are free because He has set us free!*

# DAY 36

## THE IMPORTANCE OF LOYALTY

Naomi's husband had died. Her sons had married - and both her sons were also killed, leaving her with nothing. She decided to return to Bethlehem, broken and destitute, in search of food.

Naomi said goodbye to her daughters-in-law. One of them, Ruth, refused to return to her home in Moab and abandon Naomi:

"Don't urge me to leave you or to turn back from you. Where you go I will go, and where you stay I will stay. Your people will be my people and your God my God." (Ruth 1 v 16)

What incredible loyalty! Naomi was grateful, but she couldn't quite show it. She was bitter: anyone who had lost their husband and both sons would be grieving. Yet still, Ruth stayed with her. That fierce loyalty would not be dissuaded by understandable sadness.

Ruth didn't abandon her mother-in-law, even living in the nation of Israel - about which she knew so little.

God rewarded Ruth's faith and determination. She married a man called Boaz. They had a son called Obed - and Obed was the grandfather of King David. Jesus Christ himself was born of that line.

Ruth became one of only two women in the Bible to have an entire book of the Bible devoted to her.

Why is the book of Ruth so important as to be part of the Bible? She didn't prophesy, or write songs, or tell the history of the Jewish nation, or chronicle Jesus' life, or evangelise the lost.

I believe it's because Ruth did three things.

She obeyed God. She was loyal. She was kind.

Those qualities go a very, very long way indeed.

# DAY 37

## WHERE IS YOUR FOCUS?

Have you ever tried to walk in a straight line, whilst keeping your eyes closed? It's difficult: you need to be looking where you're headed. Otherwise, you'll veer off course or walk into an unexpected lamp-post. Painful.

When we look at something, we focus on it. Have your eyes ever lingered too long looking at something you shouldn't? Christians struggle with all sorts of things: whether it's lustful thoughts, or simply seeing something and wanting it. The Ten Commandments instruct us not to do those things.

When we focus on something, it can become an obsession. We start to zone out other things. That's why it's so important to ensure that our focus is on our daily walk with God.

1 Corinthians 9 v 24 - 25 describes it like this: "Do you not know that in a race all the runners run, but only one gets the prize? Run in such a way as to get the prize. Everyone who competes in the games goes into strict training. They do it to get a crown that will not last, but we do it to get a crown that will last forever."

How do we do that? How do we get the prize? The answer is very simple, and it's found in Hebrews 12 v 1: "Let us fix our eyes on Jesus, the author and perfecter of our faith". When your focus is right, your walk with God will follow.

# DAY 38

## CONQUERING DEATH

*"I will deliver this people from the power of the grave; I will redeem them from death. Where, O death, are your plagues? Where, O grave, is your destruction?" - Hosea 13 v 14*

Unless Jesus returns, we're all going to die eventually. Hebrews 9 v 23 makes it clear that it's an experience which happens to all of us in due course.

The fear of death is real, especially for those in the world who do not know Jesus as their Lord.

I just want to remind you today of the incredible power of Jesus' death and resurrection. When Jesus died, the temple veil - the thick curtain which separated the Holy of Holies (God's presence) from the rest of the temple - was torn in two from top to bottom. In the Old Testament, only the High Priest was allowed to enter the Holy of Holies - and just once a year, at that.

As Jesus died for the forgiveness of sins, the barrier between God and humanity was lifted so that our sins could now be forgiven. We no longer required a temple veil or separation between God and His people.

And when Jesus rose from the dead, life's greatest certainty was conquered. That one event was so earth-shattering that the entirety of human history is split into two parts: everything that happened before, and everything that happened after. The Old Covenant [pact between God and humanity] and the New Covenant. God never changes, but the nature of the relationship between Him and us did.

There's a sense of incredible triumph which words can't possibly express. In the fight between good and evil, we know the ending. We know that our God wins.

When you read the words of 1 Corinthians 15 v 55 - 57, you might want to read them in your head or speak them out loud. Either way, do so with conviction because death has been utterly defeated thanks to the sacrifice made by Jesus on our behalf. There can never be any greater gift than that.

"Where, O death, is your victory? Where, O death, is your sting? The sting of death is sin, and the power of sin is the law. But thanks be to God! He gives us the victory through our Lord Jesus Christ."

# DAY 39

## TAKE A MOMENT

Breathe. For the last 38 days, I've tried to encourage you. I've tried to reassure you, to motivate you, and above all to inspire you to believe that God can make all things work together for good.

There's a lot of doing. Christianity isn't a noun. It's a verb. It's something we put into practice every single day of our lives because being a Christian is to be sent on a never-ending mission on behalf of Almighty God.

In the world there's a concept of work-life balance. In the Bible, it's about balancing work with rest - God's rest.

Right at the start of the Bible (and that's a hint - if it's right at the very beginning it might be important), in Genesis 2 v 3 we're told that on the seventh day God "rested from all the work of creating that He had done".

Exodus 20 v 9 - 10 tells us that we should follow that principle: "Six days you shall labour and do all your work, but the seventh day is a sabbath to the Lord your God."

Work is important (it's something we're supposed to do), but so is resting. I'm not suggesting that we need to become so rigid about taking a break that we forget to help those around us when they're in need. The Pharisees became so legalistic that they had a go at

Jesus for daring to heal a man on the Sabbath. Jesus gave them short shrift: the mission of helping the sick and reaching the lost trumps the notion of strict observance of a day of rest.

Nevertheless, as human beings we're designed to need rest.

Take a breather. Don't feel guilty about having a little 'me' time either, just relaxing and unwinding.

Don't underestimate the refreshing power of taking some time out of your day to spend a little time with God either.

***Today, why not read Hebrews chapter 4, which talks about entering into God's rest?***

# DAY 40

## 40 DAYS IN THE DESERT

In Matthew Chapter 4, Jesus was led into the desert. After 40 days in the desert, the devil appeared to him three times to test him.

Each time, Jesus responded by quoting a passage of scripture showing why the temptation was inaccurate. Each time, Jesus said "It is written..."

Jesus, who is by His very nature God, didn't need to quote the Old Testament. But by doing so, he showed us the way to resist temptation. He showed us that whenever we are tempted, the Bible - God's Word - is the best way to put that temptation back into its place.

Imagine spending 40 days and 40 nights in the desert. After that, you're not likely to be at your best. You might be hungry, desperate for human company, tired and angry.

Will we be tempted when things are going incredibly well, or will we be tempted at our weakest point? Frankly, I think the enemy is strategic enough to go for us in our weakness. That's what he did to Jesus.

Fortunately,  because Jesus endured that temptation, we read in Hebrews 4 v 15 that "We do not have a high priest who is unable to empathize with our weaknesses, but we have one who has been tempted in every way, just as we are - yet he did not sin."

After Jesus resisted the temptation, that's when His ministry began.

All that time in the desert must be lonely. We may not spend time in the Sahara Desert, but we have deserts of our own. The times in life where we feel dry, or that everything seems barren and meaningless.

Maybe that's been your experience of 2020 so far. I'm sure that has been the case for very many people.

It's probably a safe assumption (though it's not explicitly stated) that Jesus spent that time in prayer: prayer and fasting tend to go together in the Bible, and part of the purpose of Jesus' time in the desert was to teach us today.

If that's the situation you're in, how are you spending your '40 days in the desert'? At least it's not the 40 years the Israelites spent wandering through the desert, waiting for their promised land "flowing with milk and honey".

Those desert times are bearable partly because we know that there is a promise at the other side. There is an oasis. In John 7 v 38, Jesus promises us this:

"Let anyone who is thirsty come to me and drink. 38 Whoever believes in me, as Scripture has said, rivers of living water will flow from within them."

Do you thirst for that living water? Are you seeking God's hope in these troubled times?

Throughout the Bible, water is symbolic of life. When we're baptised, as we go under the water we 'die' to our sin and begin our new life in Christ as we come up again.

Isaiah 44 v 3 says "I will pour water on the thirsty land, and streams on the dry ground".

Maybe you're starting to feel the first little drops of rain after a drought. Those little drops

Be encouraged. There's an excitement, a hope for the future - are we ready to move into a new era?

Do not despise the day of small beginnings!